INVASIVE SPECIES

IN INFOGRAPHICS

Enviro Graphics

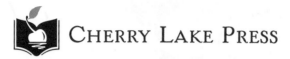

Published in the United States of America by Cherry Lake Publishing Group
Ann Arbor, Michigan
www.cherrylakepublishing.com

Reading Adviser: Marla Conn, MS, Ed., Literacy specialist, Read-Ability, Inc.
Photo Credits: ©Shutterstock, 0; ©Shutterstock, 1; ©Shutterstock, 7; ©Shutterstock, 9; ©Shutterstock, 10; ©Shutterstock, 11; ©Shutterstock, 13; ©Elionas/Pixabay, 16; ©Shutterstock, 17; ©200degrees/Pixabay, 19; ©OpenClipart-Vectors/Pixabay, 19; ©Shutterstock, 19; ©Clker-Free-Vector-Images/Pixabay, 20; ©Shutterstock, 20; ©Shutterstock, 21; ©Shutterstock, 22; ©Shutterstock, 23; ©Shutterstock, 24; ©Shutterstock, 26; ©Shutterstock, 27; ©Shutterstock, 28; ©Shutterstock, 29; ©iStockphoto/Getty Images, 30

Cherry Lake Press is an imprint of Cherry Lake Publishing Group.

Library of Congress Cataloging-in-Publication Data has been filed and is available at catalog.loc.gov

Cherry Lake Publishing Group would like to acknowledge the work of the
Partnership for 21st Century Learning, a Network of Battelle for Kids. Please
visit http://www.battelleforkids.org/networks/p21 for more information.

Printed in the United States of America
Corporate Graphics

TABLE OF CONTENTS

What Are Invasive Species?

Living things have certain areas they thrive in. These are called their natural ranges. Sometimes a plant, animal, or **pathogen** is moved. They can be transported on purpose or by accident. Then they have a new range. Once there, they can take over. When this happens, they're called invasive species. Invasives harm the local **ecosystem**. Other plants and animals can die off. Invasives can also cause damage to people's homes and crops. This damage costs a lot of money to fix. As people learn more about invasives, they find ways to prevent them and stop them from spreading.

NATIVE VS. EXOTIC VS. INVASIVE

Native
Historically from a certain area

Coexists with other species

Non-native/Exotic

Comes from a different area

Able to live in the new area

Cannot coexist with other species

Invasive

CHAPTER 1

A World with Invasive Species

Invasive species can spread naturally. This happens very slowly over time. Human activity has sped up the process. Today, humans travel across the globe every day. They move invasive species with them.

HOW SPECIES SPREAD

Naturally

- Carried by animals
- Carried in water
- Blown by wind

Accidentally

- Carried on the outside of a boat
- Hidden in crates and boxes shipped around the world
- Spread on the bottom of shoes or tires

Purposefully

- Unwanted pets released into the wild
- Discarded houseplants or decorative gardens that spread

MOST COMMON WAYS AQUATIC SPECIES SPREAD

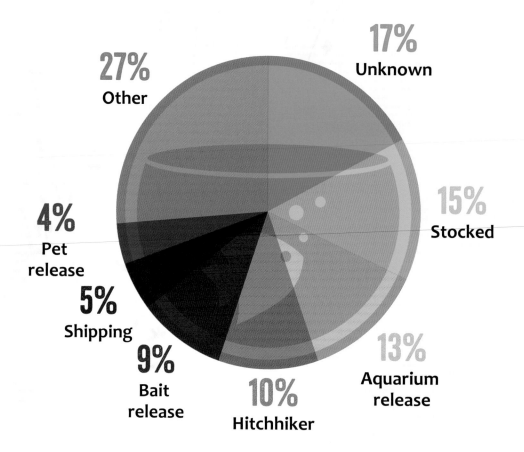

27% Other

17% Unknown

15% Stocked

4% Pet release

5% Shipping

9% Bait release

10% Hitchhiker

13% Aquarium release

2019, U.S. Geological Survey

INVASIVES FACTS

Released pet goldfish have grown as big as **DINNER PLATES**.

Dory from *Finding Dory* is an escaped aquarium fish. She could **BECOME INVASIVE**.

The aquatic plant hydrilla is invasive to the United States. It is named after the Greek **SEA MONSTER** Hydra.

TIMELINE OF INVASIVE SPECIES

3–5 million years ago:
Predators come from South America. They move to North America. They kill off many species.

20,000 years ago:
Early humans move across North America. They spread diseases and animals.

1500s–1700s:
Europeans travel across the world. They bring some species on purpose. This includes pigs. Others are brought by accident, including rats.

1800s–1900s:

North America's population grows.
People travel across rivers and lakes.
Many invasive species enter the waters.

1900s:

Major pest control efforts
go wrong. Many predators
escape and spread.

Today:

Governments, groups, and volunteers join
together. They work to prevent invasive species.
They also manage and **eradicate** invaders.

CHAPTER 2

What Makes a Species Invasive?

Many species are moved into new ranges. They do not all become invasive. There are certain **traits** that help with invasion. A species might have some, but not all, of these traits.

COMMON INVASIVE SPECIES TRAITS

- Grows quickly
- Has many babies
- Able to travel
- Can eat many different things
- Lives in groups
- Does well near humans

HOW THEY HARM

Other Species

- Changing habitat so it is not livable for native species
- **Displacement**
- Competition for food, water, and living space
- Predation
- Causing disease

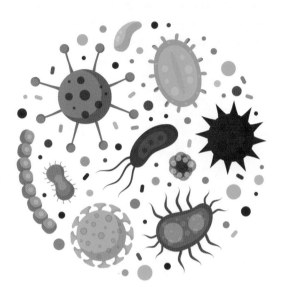

Humans

- Causing disease
- Damaging crops, water, and air quality
- Costing money to control, repair damage, and replace lost goods

SPECIES

European Wild Rabbit

- Introduced to Australia, New Zealand, and South Africa
- Has babies at a young age
- Massive damage to plants and crops
- Brought as domesticated animals; invaded as fast as 220 miles (354 kilometers) per year
- Has displaced small mammal species, leading to extinctions

Asian Carp

- Four different species
- Brought to United States for research
- Invaded major U.S. waterways
- Has many babies
- Predators; some can eat up to 40 percent of their body weight per day
- Driving prey and plants to extinction

Kudzu

- Introduced to southern United States
- Fast growth; can grow more than 60 feet (18 meters) in one season
- Can spread 2,500 acres (1,012 hectares) per year
- Crowds out native species

Chytrid Fungus

- Infectious fungal pathogen
- Spread by human activity
- Spores spread easily through water or direct contact
- By 2019, had caused declines in nearly 500 amphibian species; 90 have gone extinct

14

TIMELINE OF SPECIES

 1859 European wild rabbits are brought from southwest Europe to Victoria, Australia.

 1876 Kudzu is brought to the United States from Japan for the World's Fair. It becomes popular as a garden plant.

 Early 1900s Chytrid fungus spreads from eastern Asia.

 1910 European wild rabbits have expanded to full range.

 1940s Farmers begin planting kudzu. It feeds animals and helps with **soil erosion**.

 1963 Asian carp are brought from Eastern Asia to the southern United States.

 1966 Asian carp escape into local waters in Arkansas.

 1972 The U.S. Department of Agriculture declares kudzu a weed. It spreads across millions of acres.

 1990s Asian carp invade the Mississippi River Basin.

 1998 Scientists find out chytrid is causing massive die-offs of amphibians.

INVASIVE SPECIES HOT SPOTS

Eastern United States

Invasive: Emerald ash borer

Introduction: 2002

Method: Possibly came from wood packaging materials from northeastern Asia

Effect: Young beetles live inside trees and have killed hundreds of millions of native ash trees as of 2019.

Hawaii

Invasive: Southern house mosquito

Introduction: 1826

Method: Brought by accident through human activity

Effect: Avian malaria was spread by this invasive mosquito, driving several native bird species to extinction.

The Mediterranean Sea

Invasive: *Caulerpa taxifolia* (seaweed)

Introduction: 1980s

Method: Possibly released from an aquarium in Monaco

Effect: Seaweed is spreading across the seafloor, suffocating natural seabeds.

Guam

Invasive: Brown tree snake

Introduction: 1940s–1950s

Method: Hitchhikers on a U.S. military plane

Effect: Snakes drove their food, the island country's native birds, to extinction or near-extinction.

Lake Victoria, Africa

Invasive: Nile perch

Introduction: 1954

Method: Stocked to help replenish fish populations

Effect: As a strong predator and competitor for food, Nile perch had driven more than 200 native fish species to extinction by the early 1990s.

CHAPTER 3

Damage Done

Invasive species damage ecosystems. Unhealthy ecosystems cannot support life. Native plants and animals become threatened.

Islands are particularly vulnerable to invasives. Islands are home to many unique plants and animals. These native species are found nowhere else. They have nowhere to go if an invasive arrives. Invasives can cause a lot of damage to island biodiversity.

For humans, invasive species can cost billions of dollars. Replacing lost goods and paying for removal is expensive.

THREATS TO BIODIVERSITY

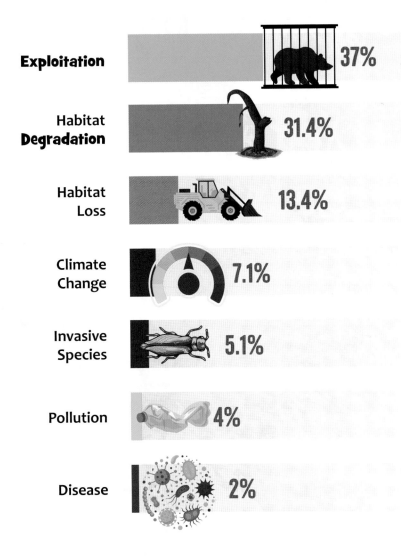

Exploitation 37%

Habitat **Degradation** 31.4%

Habitat Loss 13.4%

Climate Change 7.1%

Invasive Species 5.1%

Pollution 4%

Disease 2%

2014, World Wildlife Fund

INVASIVES FACTS

The number of invasive species **DOUBLED** between 1970 and 2020.

Since 2018, nearly **20%** of Earth's surface is at risk of invasive species. Places where people travel often are particularly threatened.

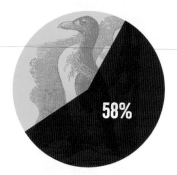

30% of U.S. species protected by the Endangered Species Act are threatened by invasives as of 2014.

58% of modern extinctions of vertebrate species are linked to invasive predators according to a 2016 report.

ISLANDS

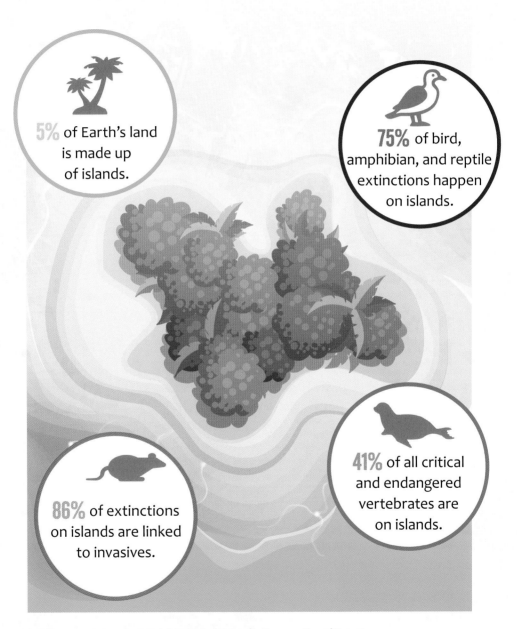

5% of Earth's land is made up of islands.

75% of bird, amphibian, and reptile extinctions happen on islands.

86% of extinctions on islands are linked to invasives.

41% of all critical and endangered vertebrates are on islands.

2017, International Union for Conservation of Nature

COST OF INVASIVE SPECIES

Damage

- Replacing lost goods
- Health costs
- Building repairs

Management

- Tracking
- Removal

TOTAL SPENT ON DAMAGE AND MANAGEMENT

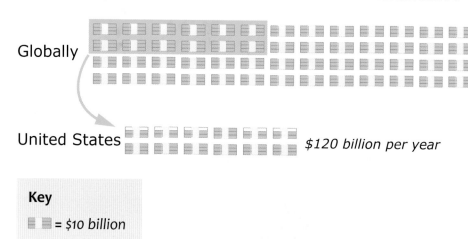

Globally

United States — $120 billion per year

Key

= $10 billion

COST TO THE UNITED STATES

Every year since 2000, invasive rats destroy close to **$20 BILLION** worth of grain and property.

Non-native species in the Great Lakes cost more than **$100 MILLION** in damages and management a year, as of 2016.

The Asian longhorned beetle cost **$373 MILLION** in eradication efforts between 1997 and 2010.

Since 2012, invasive insects cause **$13 BILLION** in agricultural losses each year.

$14 TRILLION PER YEAR

2019, Centre for Agriculture and Bioscience International; 2013, European Commission; 2012, U.S. Fish & Wildlife Service

CHAPTER 4

Controlling Invasives

There are several ways to prevent and control invasive species. Many methods need manpower, money, and several years to work. There are success stories from around the world. People can do many things in their daily lives to help with invasive species.

CONTROL METHODS

Prevention

Goal: Keep invasive species out.

Cost: Cheapest

Requires: Education, monitoring

Eradication

Goal: Remove all invasive species.

Cost: Very expensive

Requires: Many people to do work; many years of work

Chemical Control

Goal: Use herbicides, pesticides, and other chemicals to control invasives.

Cost: Not too expensive

Requires: A closed aquatic habitat, such as a lake; a good understanding of the chemicals so native species are not killed

Biological Control

Goal: Introduce a predator or disease to control invasives.

Cost: Expensive

Requires: Many people to do work; a good understanding of the predator or disease so it doesn't get out of control

Mechanical Control

Goal: Use machines or people to remove invasives by hand.

Cost: Very expensive

Requires: Many people to do work; a lot of time spent working

Ecosystem Management

Goal: Use natural methods, such as wildfire, to control invasives.

Cost: Not too expensive

Requires: Many people to do work; a good understanding of an ecosystem

SUCCESS STORIES

Tsetse Fly

Introduction: Príncipe in the Gulf of Guinea, 1825

Method: Mechanical control

Notes: Flies carried sleeping sickness. They were eradicated between 1910 and 1914 by 300 workers.

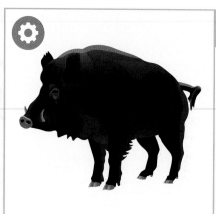

Wild Boar

Introduction: West Virginia, 1971

Method: Mechanical control

Notes: Hunters can take as many boars as they want during hunting season; populations are better controlled than in neighboring states.

[21ST CENTURY SKILLS LIBRARY]

Sea Lamprey

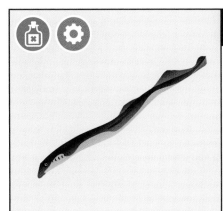

Introduction: Great Lakes, 1920s

Method: Chemical control, mechanical control

Notes: As of 2019, sea lamprey are being successfully controlled. Native fish are doing well.

Cottony Cushion Scale

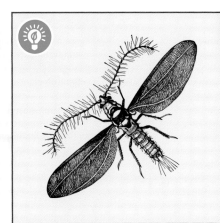

Introduction: California, 1868

Method: Biological control

Notes: These invasive insects attack citrus trees. A predator beetle was brought from Australia to help control them in 1890.

CONTROL METHODS

Mechanical

Biological

Chemical

PREVENTING SPREAD

Clean, drain, and dry all boats: the **142 MILLION** Americans who go boating each year can help prevent aquatic hitchhikers.

Don't move firewood more than **50 MILES** (80 km) to prevent the spread of insects.

Use **NATIVE PLANTS** in your garden: native plants require less water, pesticides, and maintenance.

Clean hiking and fishing gear to prevent accidental spread: since 2017, **101.6 MILLION** Americans enjoy hiking, fishing, hunting, and other nature activities.

Do not release a pet or plant into the wild: find a friend or **ANIMAL SHELTER**.

VOLUNTEER AT ONE OF AMERICA'S...

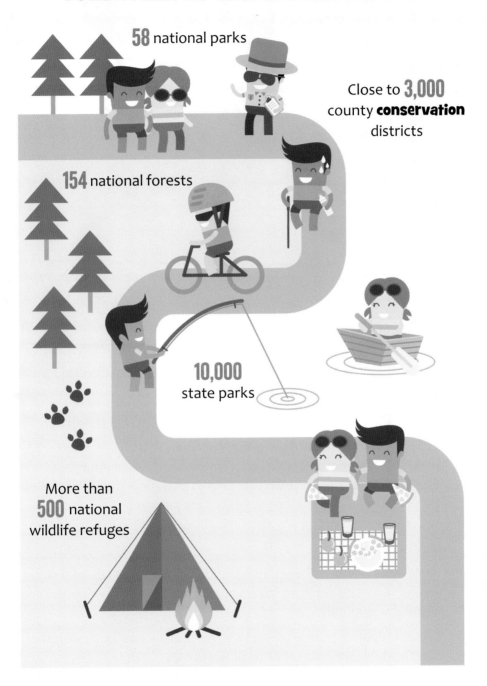

58 national parks

Close to **3,000** county **conservation** districts

154 national forests

10,000 state parks

More than **500** national wildlife refuges

Activity

LEARN YOUR SPECIES

You can be on the lookout for invasive species. First, you have to learn about what grows and lives in your area.

1. Visit your library and check out local field guides. These will tell you about native plants and animals.

2. Have an adult help you get a list of invasive species in your area. They can get one from your State Department of Natural Resources. Use the internet to find their contact information.

3. Use the field guide and invasives list to identify each species. Are they native or invasive?

4. Look at the plants and animals around your home or school. For each new species you find, take a photograph. Write down notes on where it was found.

5. You can report any invasive species you find. Get in touch with the person who helped you at Natural Resources.

Learn More

BOOKS

Howell, Izzi. *Biodiversity.* New York, NY: Crabtree Publishing, 2019.

Hunt, Santana. *Attack of the Asian Carp!* New York, NY: Gareth Stevens Publishing, 2017.

Levy, Janey. *How Invasive Species Take Over.* New York, NY: Gareth Stevens Publishing, 2020.

WEBSITES

Green Invaders
https://kids.nationalgeographic.com/explore/science/green-invaders

Ten of the World's Most Invasive Species
https://www.earthrangers.com/top-10/ten-of-the-worlds-most-invasive-species/

Invasive Species—What You Can Do
https://www.fws.gov/invasives/what-you-can-do.html

BIBLIOGRAPHY

Encyclopædia Britannica. "Invasive Species." Last modified February 7, 2019. https://www.britannica.com/science/invasive-species

Encyclopedia of Life. "Invasive Species." https://eol.org/docs/discover/invasive-species

U.S. Department of Agriculture. "What Are Invasive Species?" https://www.invasivespeciesinfo.gov/what-are-invasive-species

U.S. Fish and Wildlife Service. "Frequently Asked Questions about Invasive Species." Last modified November 20, 2012. https://www.fws.gov/invasives/faq.html#q3

U.S. Geological Survey. "NAS Graphs and Charts: All Introduced Aquatic Species in the US." Last modified December 18, 2019. https://nas.er.usgs.gov/graphs/All.aspx

GLOSSARY

coexist (koh-eg-ZISTS) peacefully live at the same time or place

conservation (kon-sur-VAY-shuhn) the protection of animals, plants, and natural resources, such as water

degradation (deg-ruh-DAY-shuhn) the process of breaking down or damaging something

displacement (dis-PLAYS-ment) to force people or animals out of where they live

ecosystem (EE-koh-sis-tuhm) a community of living things and their environment

eradicate (ih-RA-dih-kaytE) to completely remove or destroy something in a particular area

exploitation (eks-ploy-TAY-shuhn) the use of a resource to make money while ignoring any damage being done

pathogen (PATH-oh-jen) a tiny organism or virus that causes disease

predators (PRED-uh-turz) animals that kill and eat other animals for food

soil erosion (SOYL ee-ROH-zhuhn) the wearing away of soil by wind and water

traits (TRAYTS) qualities or characteristics that makes a living thing unique

INDEX

ABOUT THE AUTHOR

Renae Gilles is an author, editor, and ecologist from the Pacific Northwest. She has a bachelor's degree in humanities from Evergreen State College and a master's in biology from Eastern Washington University. Renae and her husband live in Washington with their two daughters, Edith and Louisa.